W9-AYA-925

The Scientists Behind

Space

Eve Hartman and Wendy Meshbesher

Chicago, Illinois

www.heinemannraintree.com
Visit our website to find out more information about Heinemann-Raintree books.

To order:
☎ Phone 888-454-2279
🖥 Visit www.heinemannraintree.com to browse our catalog and order online.

© 2011 Raintree
an imprint of Capstone Global Library, LLC
Chicago, Illinois

Edited by Andrew Farrow, Adam Miller, and Diyan Leake
Designed by Philippa Jenkins
Original illustrations © Capstone Global Library Limited 2011
Illustrated by Capstone Global Library Limited
Picture research by Hannah Taylor
Originated by Capstone Global Library Limited
Printed in the United States of America by Worzalla Publishing

14 13 12 11 10
10 9 8 7 6 5 4 3 2 1

Library of Congress Cataloging-in-Publication Data
Hartman, Eve.
  The scientists behind space / Eve Hartman and Wendy Meshbesher.
    p. cm.—(Sci-hi. Scientists)
  Includes bibliographical references and index.
  ISBN 978-1-4109-4049-0 (hc)—ISBN 978-1-4109-4056-8 (pb) 1. Astronomers—Juvenile literature. 2. Astronomy—History—Juvenile literature. I. Meshbesher, Wendy. II. Title.
  QB35.H37 2011
  520.92—dc22   2010031264

Acknowledgments
The author and publishers are grateful to the following for permission to reproduce copyright material: Alamy Images p. **7** (© World History Archive); The Art Archive p. **10** (Galleria degli Uffizi Florence/Gianni Dagli Orti); Corbis pp. **8** (Paul Almasy), **11** (Roger Ressmeyer), **15** (George Steinmetz), **16** (Najlah Feanny-Hicks), **20** (Bettmann), **25** (Science Faction/Peter Ginter), **31** (Reuters/Charles W. Luzier), **37** (Xinhua Press/XinHua/Li Xueren); Getty Images pp. **9** (Time Life Pictures/Mansell), **14** (NY Daily News Archive/Linda Cataffo), **33** (AFP/Sylvie Kauffmann); NASA **contents page** top (JPL/Space Science Institute), **contents page** bottom, pp. **6** (Courtesy of Howard McCallon), **17** (H. Hammel, MIT), **18** (Ames Research Center), **19** (International Astronomical Union), **21**, **23** top, **26** (TRW), **29** (JPL/Space Science Institute), **28** (ESA/JPL/Arizona State University), **32** (Goddard Space Flight Center), **34**, **35**, **36** (Johnson Space Center Collection), **38**, **39** (Mars Exploration Rover Mission), **41**; Science Photo Library pp. **4** (David Parker), **12** (CCI Archives), **23** bottom, **24** (American Institute of Physics/Emilio Segre Visual Archives); shutterstock background images and design elements throughout. Main cover photograph of Ellen Ochoa reproduced with permission of NASA; inset cover photograph of a comet reproduced with permission of NASA.

The publisher would like to thank literary consultant Marla Conn and content consultant Suzy Gazlay for their assistance in the preparation of this book.

Every effort has been made to contact copyright holders of material reproduced in this book. Any omissions will be rectified in subsequent printings if notice is given to the publisher.

Disclaimer
All the Internet addresses (URLs) given in this book were valid at the time of going to press. However, due to the dynamic nature of the Internet, some addresses may have changed, or sites may have changed or ceased to exist since publication. While the author and publisher regret any inconvenience this may cause readers, no responsibility for any such changes can be accepted by either the author or the publisher.

Contents

Space 4

The Copernican Revolution 8

Astronomy Today 14

Is Pluto a Planet? 18

Stars and Galaxies 20

Telescopes and Other Tools 26

New Discoveries 28

Exploring Space 34

The Space Race 36

Timeline 42

Quick Quiz 44

Glossary 45

Find Out More 46

Index 48

Which of Saturn's moons has volcanic eruptions? Find out on page 29!

Where are these astronauts? Turn to page 41 to find out!

Some words are shown in bold, **like this**. These words are explained in the glossary. You will find important information and definitions underlined, like this.

SPACE

Have you ever stared at a starry sky at night? Have you wondered what space is like, and what is Earth's place in the universe? If you have done these things, you are not alone. People have been wondering about space for thousands of years. Legends about Earth, the stars, and space date back to ancient times. Today, scientific facts and theories explain much about space. In this book you will learn about the scientists who studied space and about space explorers.

This photo shows the tracks of stars above the radio telescope at Jodrell Bank in the United Kingdom.

OLD IDEAS

When the Sun sets on towns and cities today, people turn on electric lights to continue working and playing, and to find their way. Hundreds of years ago, people relied much more on the lights in the sky. The ancient Mayans, Babylonians, and Greeks all studied the skies carefully. They recognized patterns of change, such as the way some stars appear only at certain times of the year.

Although ancient peoples may not have explained space correctly, they did apply their knowledge to help them lead their lives. Farmers studied the stars to know when to plant and harvest crops. Sailors studied the stars to find their way at night.

RADIO TELESCOPES

Today, scientists study the sky with many kinds of **telescopes**. A telescope makes distant objects appear closer. Most telescopes form images with light, the way the eye does. **Radio telescopes** form images from radio waves. Stars release radio waves and other kinds of **radiation** as well as light.

Chichén Itzá was a Mayan city that thrived about 1,500 years ago. The building shown here is part of a pyramid for observing changes of the seasons. The sides of the pyramid face north, south, east, and west. On the first days of spring and autumn, the Sun casts shadows that look like a snake slithering down the pyramid's steps.

CONSTELLATIONS

On a clear, dark night, you might see thousands of stars—some bright, others very faint. The stars appear to be scattered unevenly across the sky. To make sense of the stars, ancient peoples grouped them into patterns called **constellations**. Astronomers today recognize 88 constellations. Most of these were known to the ancient Greeks and Romans.

You can find constellations by playing "connect the dots" in the night sky. Here is part of the constellation Orion.

Orion's belt

THE THREE MARYS

Different cultures organize stars in different ways. In South America, the stars of Orion's belt are called the Three Marys after three women named Mary in the Bible. The stars appear in the northern sky and can help people find their way at night.

ONLY FROM EARTH

Astronomers and star gazers continue to study constellations, the way people did in ancient times. We now know, however, that the constellations only look the way they do from our viewpoint on Earth.

Consider the three stars that make up the belt of the constellation Orion, shown above. The stars look very close together, but that's just the way they look from our position in space.

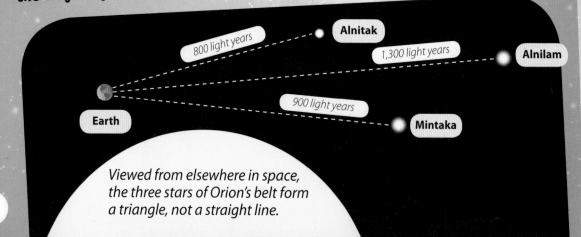

Alnitak

800 light years

1,300 light years

Alnilam

900 light years

Earth

Mintaka

Viewed from elsewhere in space, the three stars of Orion's belt form a triangle, not a straight line.

PTOLEMY

Claudius Ptolemaeus—better known as Ptolemy—was a citizen of ancient Rome who lived in Egypt about two thousand years ago. Up until the 1700s, people considered his book, the *Almagest*, to be the best source of information about objects in the sky. The book described many constellations. It also predicted changes in the positions of stars and the planets from season to season.

Ptolemy's work was useful, but it did not describe the universe accurately. In Ptolemy's model, Earth was a fixed point in space. The Sun, stars, and planets moved around Earth. After Ptolemy's time, new tools, such as the telescope, helped scientists disprove Ptolemy's ideas.

This painting shows Ptolemy holding a simple model of the universe with the Earth at the center.

The COPERNICAN REVOLUTION

Day after day, the Sun appears to rise in the east and set in the west. It seems as though the Sun **revolves**, or moves around, the planet Earth. Indeed, for hundreds of years people believed this idea. In 1543, Nicolaus Copernicus proposed that it was Earth, not the Sun, that moves. The fact that Earth moves through space was one of the most important scientific discoveries in history.

NICOLAUS COPERNICUS

LIVED: 1473–1543

NATIONALITY: Polish

FAMOUS FOR: Proposing that planets revolve around the Sun, not Earth

DID YOU KNOW? Copernicus studied mathematics, law, and medicine. Astronomy was almost like a hobby for him.

In Copernicus's model of the universe, Earth and other planets revolve around the Sun.

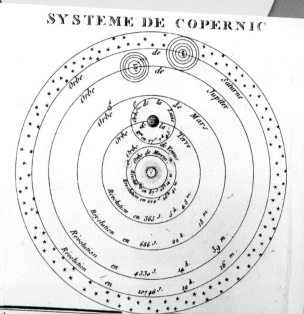

SYSTEME DE COPERNIC

Objects in the sky are sometimes called heavenly spheres or heavenly bodies. Copernicus's book, *On the Revolutions of the Heavenly Spheres*, follows the style of Ptolemy and uses the same data. Yet Copernicus's model of the universe was different in one key way: <u>the planets revolve around the Sun, not around Earth</u>. Copernicus also listed the order of the known planets around the Sun.

Copernicus inspired other scientists to view the universe in new ways, with the Sun at the center of a large system of planets and other objects. He began a series of discoveries about space that we now call the Copernican Revolution.

THE WANDERERS

The word *planet* comes from the Greek for "wanderer." From night to night, the planets appear to wander about the stars in the sky. This wandering motion was evidence for the idea that the Sun was in the center. If the planets revolved around Earth, they should not appear to wander.

ASTROLOGY and ASTRONOMY

Astronomy is the scientific study of space. Don't confuse the term with astrology.

Astrology, which is not a science, is concerned with how stars might affect people's personalities and fate.

EVIDENCE

One hundred years after Copernicus died, the idea of an Earth-centered system was still widely accepted. Among those who believed in the old idea were officials of the Catholic Church, which was very powerful at the time.

The Italian scientist Galileo Galilei thought otherwise. He based his ideas on **evidence**, which is facts that can be observed. Galileo's evidence came in part from the powerful telescopes he built. One important piece of evidence that Galileo discovered was that the planet Venus has **phases**, just like the phases of the Moon. Phases are the changing shapes of a planet or moon as viewed from Earth. The shapes do not really change.

GALILEO GALILEI

LIVED: 1564–1642

NATIONALITY: Italian

FAMOUS FOR: Proving that the Sun was at the center of a system of planets

DID YOU KNOW? Galileo played the flute. His father was a famous musician.

"Galileo, perhaps more than any other single person, was responsible for the birth of modern science.... Galileo was one of the first to argue that man could hope to understand how the world works, and moreover, that we could do this by observing the real world."

Stephen Hawking (see pages 30–31)

Galileo used the evidence he gathered to argue that the Sun, not Earth, was the center of a system in space. The Catholic Church forced Galileo to take back his ideas. For punishment, he was forced to spend the rest of his life under house arrest.

The Galileo *space probe was named in Galileo's honor. It was the first spacecraft to orbit Jupiter.*

GALILEO'S ACCOMPLISHMENTS

- Built telescopes that could magnify images 30 times their natural size
- Discovered four moons of Jupiter, now called the Galilean moons
- Observed the rings of Saturn, craters on the Moon, and sunspots
- Designed improvements for a thermometer, compass, and a clock with a pendulum (weight to operate it)
- Proposed that gravity caused all objects to speed up equally

THE ROLE OF GRAVITY

What keeps the planets in their orbits (paths) around the Sun? The British scientist Isaac Newton (1643–1727) showed that the answer involves two important principles: **gravity** and **inertia**. As Newton explained, <u>gravity is an attractive force between any two objects</u>. On Earth's surface, the force of gravity pulls everything downward. The Sun, however, is by far the most massive object in its neighborhood of space. Gravity pulls Earth and the other planets toward the Sun.

Inertia is the tendency of a moving object to keep moving. The planets' inertia keeps them moving forward, while gravity bends their paths toward the Sun. As a result, each planet revolves around the Sun in a regular, well-defined orbit.

In the 1600s, Isaac Newton proposed three simple laws of motion. Scientists still use these laws to explain the motion of nearly every object in the universe.

KEPLER'S LAWS

The work of the German scientist Johannes Kepler (1571–1630) helped Newton develop his ideas about gravity. As Kepler explained, the shape of a planet's orbit is an ellipse, or kind of oval. Kepler also developed a mathematical formula to show that planets move fastest when they are nearest the Sun, and slowest when they are furthest away.

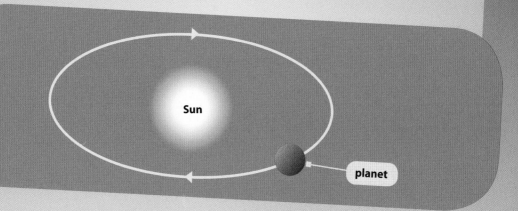

Sun

planet

GRAVITY SLINGSHOT

Imagine you are the pilot of a spaceship that is low on fuel and you need to change course quickly. If a large planet is nearby, you could try a gravity slingshot. In this technique, the spaceship enters orbit around a planet, then leaves orbit when it is heading in the proper direction. In the future, a pilot might use the planet's gravity to provide all the energy needed for the course change.

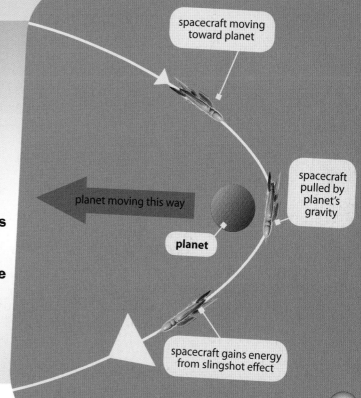

spacecraft moving toward planet

spacecraft pulled by planet's gravity

planet moving this way

planet

spacecraft gains energy from slingshot effect

ASTRONOMY TODAY

Many questions that once puzzled astronomers now have very simple answers. <u>Scientists can precisely identify the positions of Earth and the other planets around the Sun</u>. By applying this knowledge, they can explain such events as day and night, the changing seasons, and eclipses. Eclipses occur when the position of one object in space, such as Earth or the Moon, blocks the view of another object.

Yet many facts about the universe remain to be discovered. Astronomers today are discovering new bodies in the distant parts of the solar system. They are also discovering planets around distant stars, and even new stars and galaxies.

NEIL DEGRASSE TYSON

BORN: 1958

NATIONALITY: American

FAMOUS FOR: Presenting astronomy to the public

DID YOU KNOW? Tyson hosted a radio program with Lynne Koplitz, a stand-up comic. The aim of the program was to make science fun and interesting for everyone.

As a young boy, Neil DeGrasse Tyson liked to climb to the top of his apartment block and look at the Moon. He began to study astronomy on his own. By the age of 15, he was giving lectures on astronomy. Today, Tyson has a doctor's degree in astrophysics, which is the study of the physical properties of objects in space.

Tyson spends much of his time studying space. He also works hard to share his knowledge with the public. One of his jobs is director of the Hayden Planetarium in New York City. <u>A planetarium is a theater for viewing images of stars, planets, and other objects in the sky</u>. Tyson also writes popular books, hosts television shows, and speaks about space to people all over the world.

ASTRONOMY CAREERS

All professional astronomers must be experts in math as well as science. Most work for colleges, universities, or museums. People often think that they spend much of their time looking at the stars through telescopes. In fact, their time is spent mostly on analyzing data, usually with the help of computers.

YOU CAN BE AN ASTRONOMER, TOO!

Anyone can be an amateur astronomer. You don't even need a telescope! All you need to do is observe the stars, Moon, and planets that you see in the night sky. You can also visit planetariums and read about space in books, in magazines, and on the Internet. See pages 46–47 for more ideas.

An exhibit of the Big Bang (see page 30) is projected onto the floor at the Hayden Planetarium in New York City.

NEW DISCOVERIES IN THE SOLAR SYSTEM

Many planets of the solar system have been known since ancient times. However, in recent years astronomers have discovered small, far-away objects beyond Neptune, the outermost planet. They have also learned more about **asteroids**, which are rocks in space that are too small to be classified as planets.

Comets are masses of ice and dust that orbit the Sun. They are sometimes nicknamed "dirty snowballs." The record for discovering the most comets belongs to Carolyn Shoemaker, who has discovered more than 30 of them. She has also found more than 800 asteroids.

CAROLYN SHOEMAKER

BORN:	1929
NATIONALITY:	American
FAMOUS FOR:	Discovering comets
DID YOU KNOW?	Shoemaker did not begin studying astronomy until she was 51 years old.

Shoemaker finds comets and asteroids by carefully studying photos of the night sky. She enjoys the thrill of discovery. She also knows that her work is important. Comets and asteroids provide clues to how Earth formed and changed over time. Moreover, if a comet or asteroid ever collided with Earth in the future, the results could be a major disaster. Shoemaker hopes to discover knowledge that will help protect the planet.

The most famous comet she helped discover was Comet Shoemaker-Levy 9. In 1994, pieces of this comet crashed into Jupiter. The collisions were violent, showing all observers just how much damage a comet could cause if it collided with Earth.

DANGER TO EARTH?

Unlike the planets, asteroids and comets have orbits that are difficult to predict. Their small mass and size means that the gravity of nearby objects can change their movements significantly.

Scientists believe that asteroids and comets have collided with Earth in the past. A collision with an asteroid 65 million years ago is thought to have killed all the dinosaurs and many other living things on Earth.

Scientists at the National Aeronautics and Space Administration (**NASA**) watch objects near Earth very closely. In recent years, many have come close to Earth, although none dangerously close. In the future, scientists may be able to use rockets or explosives to break apart an object heading to Earth or change its course.

When pieces of a comet struck Jupiter, they launched this ring-shaped debris into Jupiter's atmosphere. Imagine the damage if the comet had struck Earth!

IS Pluto A PLANEt?

Alan Stern was the lead scientist of a NASA robotic spacecraft mission to Pluto.

For many years, scientists had identified nine planets revolving around the Sun. The ninth planet, Pluto, was also the most unusual. It was quite small, the shape of its orbit was unusually stretched, and it orbited at an odd angle to the orbits of the other planets.

Recently, however, scientists discovered that Pluto was not so unusual after all. They found many objects of similar size in orbit beyond Pluto. This led to many questions. Should these new objects be classified as planets? If not, how should Pluto be properly classified?

In 2006 the International Astronomical Union (IAU) reached a decision. A planet, they decided, needed to have cleared its neighborhood of smaller objects. Pluto and the objects beyond it were classified as dwarf planets, a new category for objects smaller than planets.

The IAU decision may be final. However, many astronomers and others disagree with the decision. Many have published articles, signed petitions, and launched campaigns to have Pluto named a planet once again.

Is Pluto a planet? YES!

"Any definition that allows a planet in one location but not another is unworkable. Take Earth. Move it to Pluto's orbit, and it will be instantly disqualified as a planet."

Alan Stern, Director of NASA's
New Horizons mission to Pluto

Is Pluto a planet? NO!

"The scientific community has realized that the classification used for Pluto for 75 years was not correct."

Gonzalo Tancredi, astronomer at the University of Uruguay

ILLINOIS'S PLUTO LAW

In the state of Illinois, Pluto remains a planet. The state government passed a law that recognizes Pluto as the ninth planet. Illinois was the birthplace of Clyde Tombaugh, the astronomer who discovered Pluto in 1930. A similar law has been proposed in New Mexico, the state where Tombaugh worked for much of his career.

DWARF PLANETS

The table on the right shows the relative size of some dwarf planets compared to Pluto. Ceres is located in the asteroid belt between Mars and Jupiter. The other dwarf planets are beyond Neptune, very far from the Sun.

Name	Size (compared to Pluto)
Ceres	41%
Haumea	62%
Makemake	75%
Pluto	100%
Eris	105%

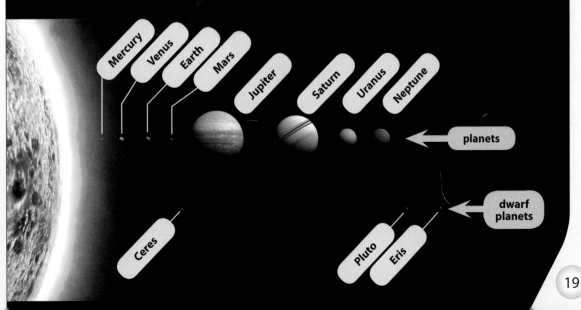

Mercury · Venus · Earth · Mars · Jupiter · Saturn · Uranus · Neptune — planets

Ceres · Pluto · Eris — dwarf planets

STARS and GALAXIES

From Earth, stars appear as tiny points of white light in the night sky. If we could view stars up close, they would appear as huge, fiery balls in space. They also have a variety of colors, including orange, red, yellow, blue, and white. Many astronomers have studied stars and tried to understand their properties. The easiest star to study is also the closest—the Sun.

CECILIA PAYNE-GAPOSCHKIN

LIVED: 1900–1979

NATIONALITY: British American

FAMOUS FOR: Discoveries about the nature of stars

DID YOU KNOW? Payne-Gaposchkin was the first person to receive a doctorate in astronomy from Harvard University.

CECILIA PAYNE-GAPOSCHKIN

Cecilia Payne-Gaposchkin began her life at a time when very few women had careers in science. She realized she wanted to be an astronomer when she was 5 years old, after watching a meteor streak across the sky. Twenty years later, she had earned a doctorate in astronomy from Harvard College **Observatory** and had published two books about the stars. Her most important discovery was that stars are made mostly of two elements: hydrogen and helium. She discovered this by carefully analyzing the light that stars emit (give off).

Payne-Gaposchkin's colleagues at Harvard treated her poorly for many years because she was a woman. Despite her brilliant work, she earned a small salary and was assigned few duties. Eventually, she was promoted to full professor. By 1956 she was in charge of the astronomy department. Her acceptance as an astronomer opened the door for other women to enter the field.

PLASMA IN STARS

On Earth, nearly all matter is in one of three states: solid, liquid, or gas. The matter of a star, however, is in a state called plasma. Plasma is like a gas, but is made of electrically charged particles. The plasma of a star exists at extremely high temperatures, much higher than ever found on Earth.

This fiery ball in space is the Sun, one of the stars that fascinated Payne-Gaposchkin.

CLASSIFYING STARS

By the early 1900s, astronomers knew that stars differed in brightness, temperature, size, color, and other properties. Then the Danish astronomer Ejnar Hertzsprung and U.S. astronomer Henry Russell discovered an interesting trend among the stars. They made a graph that showed that <u>the color of stars is related to their temperature and brightness</u>.

In this graph, most stars fall near a line that slopes down the graph. These stars are called main-sequence stars. Blue stars are the hottest and brightest of the main sequence stars. Red stars are the coolest.

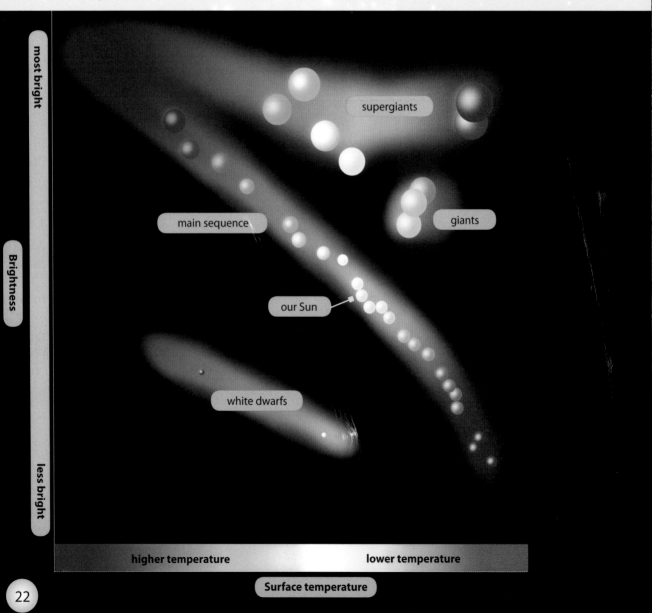

most bright

Brightness

less bright

supergiants

main sequence

giants

our Sun

white dwarfs

higher temperature   lower temperature

Surface temperature

MEET THE SUN

The Sun is an average star in many ways. It is a main-sequence star of average temperature, which gives it a yellow-orange color. It is also about halfway through its life cycle: it is about 4.6 billion years old and has about 5 billion years remaining. Then it will become a red giant, a type of large star. Life on Earth will not survive this change.

A *supernova* is an explosion of a massive star. This supernova took place in another galaxy.

A few stars plot above the main-sequence stars. They are called supergiants, and are very large stars. Other stars plot near the bottom of the graph. They are white dwarfs, which are very old, relatively small stars.

Stars are not alive, but it is helpful to think of them in terms of existing and gradually ceasing to exist. Stars form, or are "born." They change as they age, and eventually they stop burning. Understanding the life of stars was the lifetime goal of the astronomer and physicist Subrahmanyan Chandrasekhar.

SUBRAHMANYAN "CHANDRA" CHANDRASEKHAR

LIVED:	1910–1995
NATIONALITY:	Indian American
FAMOUS FOR:	Explaining how stars form and change
DID YOU KNOW?	One of Chandra's students was astronomer Carl Sagan (see page 40).

One of Chandra's conclusions was that massive stars collapsed into themselves to form an object of enormous density (mass per unit of volume). Today we call these objects **black holes**, and you will learn more about them on page 30.

GALAXIES

Looking at stars in the night sky, you might think that they are scattered evenly across the universe. This is not the case. <u>Stars bunch together in groups called **galaxies**</u>. The stars we see in the night sky belong to our local galaxy, the Milky Way. It contains over 100 billion stars, including the Sun.

How many galaxies are in the universe? Astronomers are very interested in this question. One recent estimate was 125 billion galaxies, but the number could be much larger. As everyone agrees, the universe is a very, very big place.

EDWIN HUBBLE

LIVED: 1889–1953

NATIONALITY: American

FAMOUS FOR: Identifying and classifying galaxies, describing the movement of galaxies

DID YOU KNOW? Edwin's grandfather allowed him to stay up late to look through a telescope as a treat on his eighth birthday.

Astronomers once thought that the Milky Way was the only galaxy in the universe. Edwin Hubble proved this idea was incorrect. He observed and identified several stars that were much too distant to be part of the Milky Way. He later devised a way to classify galaxies based on their appearances.

Another of his contributions, now called Hubble's law, discusses the speed at which galaxies are moving. This law helped show that the universe is constantly expanding.

THE HUBBLE SPACE TELESCOPE

Many years after Hubble died, the Hubble Space Telescope was named in his honor. Space is an ideal place for telescopes because it is beyond Earth's atmosphere, or layer of air. The atmosphere absorbs and scatters light, limiting the usefulness of telescopes on the surface of the Earth.

The Hubble Space Telescope has taken many amazing photos of distant stars and galaxies. It is scheduled to remain active until 2014, when a new space telescope will replace it.

VERA RUBIN

In the 1950s, a young American astronomer named Vera Rubin (shown below in 2004) argued that galaxies were spread unevenly across the universe. She also claimed that the stars of a spiral galaxy rotated about the center. Astronomers of the time scoffed at these ideas, yet both proved to be true.

Dr. Rubin's most surprising discovery came years later, when she studied the speeds of rotating stars. Her research suggested that the stars were affected by an invisible mass, now called **dark matter**. Scientists now think that over 90 percent of the universe is made of dark matter.

Telescopes and Other Tools

Like other scientists, astronomers depend on technology to observe objects in nature. The most important technology for astronomers is the telescope. A telescope is a tool that forms clear images of distant objects, such as distant planets, stars, and other objects in space.

Astronomers also rely on **space probes** to carry telescopes. Space probes communicate with Earth over radio waves. Messages from scientists on Earth control the probe, and messages from the probe transmit photographs and other data.

The Chandra *telescope sends data coded in radio waves to Earth. The wing-like parts are solar panels that provide energy for the telescope.*

MANY TELESCOPES

The first telescopes, like the ones Galileo used, were optical telescopes. Optical telescopes use lenses or mirrors to form images from light rays. Today, however, very powerful telescopes form images from radio waves, microwaves, or X-rays. Stars release each of these forms of energy, and each can be used to form images.

BETH BROWN

As a girl, Beth Brown (1969–2008) enjoyed conducting experiments for science fairs. She also liked science fiction stories about traveling to outer space. Later, after many years of hard work and study, she became an **astrophysicist**, which is a scientist who studies the physical properties of objects in space.

Brown eventually went to work for NASA. As part of her job, she used the *Chandra* X-ray Observatory, the most powerful telescope of its kind. This telescope orbits high above Earth and studies the X-rays emitted by exploded stars and other objects. It is named after Subrahmanyam Chandrasekhara, whom you read about on page 23.

"In school ... I liked science because I was always curious about how something worked and why something existed. Space fascinated me. I grew up watching *Star Trek*, *Star Wars*, and other shows/movies that portrayed space."

Beth Brown

NEW DISCOVERIES

With the help of space probes and telescopes, astronomers have made a huge number of discoveries about the universe. Many more will be made in the future.

DISTANT STARS AND GALAXIES

From Earth, some small regions of the night sky appear black and empty. However, these regions might actually be filled with stars that can be viewed from space.

The Hubble Space Telescope has taken amazing pictures of entire events, such as the supernova on the left. It has also photographed stars in different stages of their life cycle.

MANY MOONS

Galileo discovered the four largest moons of Jupiter. Today, scientists have identified over 60 moons around Jupiter, most of which are less than 50 kilometers (30 miles) wide. They have also found large numbers of moons around Saturn, Uranus, and Neptune. Even Pluto has three moons!

The American scientist Carolyn Porco helped discover seven of Saturn's moons. She led the imaging team for the Cassini-Huygens space probe to Saturn. Photos showed that one of the moons, named Enceladus (right), has events like volcanic eruptions. Dr. Porco and other scientists think that Enceladus could have liquid water beneath its surface. It is possible that living things could have developed in this water.

EXTRASOLAR PLANETS

For years, astronomers guessed that other stars had planets around them. In 1992 the Polish astronomer Aleksander Wolszczan and the Canadian astronomer Dale Frail announced the first extrasolar planet—a planet in orbit around a star other than the Sun. Today, scientists have found over 400 extrasolar planets. Most are gas giants, like Saturn and Jupiter. Some are smaller and more like Earth. Scientists continue to look for and study extrasolar planets. Very little is known about any of them.

THE BIG BANG

Many scientists once thought that the universe had no beginning. Edwin Hubble showed that the universe is expanding very rapidly. By assuming that this expansion has always been occurring, <u>scientists formed the theory that the universe began as an extremely small and dense particle</u>. Then, very suddenly, the particle exploded. This event is called the **Big Bang**. If the theory is correct, the Big Bang occurred over 13 billion years ago.

After the Big Bang, the universe expanded extremely rapidly. It continues expanding today.

Stephen Hawking is one of the most accomplished scientists of our time. His work has helped explain many events in the history of the universe, including the Big Bang. He has also helped define and describe black holes, which form from the explosions of very large stars. A black hole is a region of space that is so massive that nothing—not even light— can escape its gravity.

One of Hawking's ideas, now widely accepted, is that time and space have no boundary or edge. Hawking argued that the universe is expanding, but the same laws apply to all points of the universe at all times— including at the moment of the Big Bang.

Hawking has written many popular books about science. His book *A Brief History of Time* was a best seller for over four years.

Hawking's accomplishments are even more remarkable considering his health. At age 21, Hawking began suffering from a disease of the nervous system. Gradually, the disease left him almost completely paralyzed. For much of his career he has been confined to a wheelchair and used an artificial voice box to speak.

"Although there was a cloud hanging over my future, I found to my surprise that I was enjoying life in the present more than I had before."

Stephen Hawking, when his disease was first diagnosed

STEPHEN HAWKING

BORN: 1942

NATIONALITY: British

FAMOUS FOR: Studying black holes, describing and predicting the history of the universe

DID YOU KNOW? Hawking is a fan of science fiction, and has acted briefly in *Futurama*, *Star Trek: The Next Generation*, and other television programs.

NAMING THE BIG BANG

The name "Big Bang" was coined by British astronomer Fred Hoyle in 1949. But Hoyle did not believe in the theory! He may have meant the term as an insult.

In 1993, an international contest was held to rename the theory. Many entries were considered, but none were declared the winner. The judges agreed that "Big Bang" describes the theory best.

AFTER THE BIG BANG

Within a fraction of a second after the Big Bang, the universe grew to the size that the solar system is now. The tiny particles that make up matter as we know it began to form. Temperatures were extremely hot, but they gradually began to cool.

As time passed, the force of gravity began to bring together the matter within a region of space. Stars eventually formed. Hydrogen and helium are the most common elements in stars, but elements as heavy as iron can form in stars, too. <u>When a very massive star explodes—an event called a supernova—the energy is high enough to form all the elements that are heavier than iron</u>.

Stars have been forming, growing larger, and dying or exploding throughout the long history of the universe. Most scientists now believe that these processes will never end. The universe will continue expanding forever.

EVIDENCE FOR THE BIG BANG

If the Big Bang took place, then the radiation it emitted should still be present in the universe. In 1989 NASA launched the Cosmic Background Explorer (COBE) to find this radiation. COBE found exactly what the scientists were seeking! The radiation provided evidence for the Big Bang theory. It also won a Nobel Prize for the project's leaders, U.S. astrophysicists John Mather and George F. Smoot.

Astrophysicist John Mather.

The Russian physicist Andrei Sakharov was an expert on many subjects, including the military use of nuclear energy. In space science, he studied the events that occurred just after the Big Bang. He proposed that two universes formed from the Big Bang. One is the universe that we live in. The second is a universe made mostly of particles called antimatter. A particle of antimatter is just like a corresponding particle of matter, but the two particles would destroy each other if they came in contact!

ANDREI SAKHAROV

LIVED: 1921–1989

NATIONALITY: Russian

FAMOUS FOR: Describing matter and antimatter

DID YOU KNOW? In 1983 U.S. President Ronald Reagan proclaimed May 21 as National Sakharov Day. Sakharov was under arrest in the Soviet Union at the time.

POLITICAL CONTROVERSY

Andrei Sakharov urged the Soviet Union (a country that included Russia) to reduce its stockpiles of nuclear weapons and to sign treaties with the United States, its main rival. The Soviet government punished Sakharov for these views. When Sakharov won the Nobel Peace Prize in 1975, he was not allowed to leave the country to receive it.

Do you find antimatter confusing? If so, you are not alone. Antimatter cannot be easily observed and it is difficult to study and explain. Nevertheless, scientists have proved that antimatter exists.

Exploring Space

For thousands of years, space travel was only a dream. Today, astronauts of many nations travel to and from space every year. Many live for weeks or months at a time on the International Space Station.

In many ways, exploring space is science at its best. It is a quest for knowledge and adventure that everyone can benefit from. As you will discover, the quest depends on the cooperation of many different scientists, including astronauts, engineers, and biologists.

ELLEN OCHOA

Early in her career, U.S. astronaut and scientist Ellen Ochoa invented ways for machines to "see" objects. She earned three patents for her inventions. Her work impressed NASA, where she was hired to supervise a staff of 35 scientists at the Ames Research Center in California.

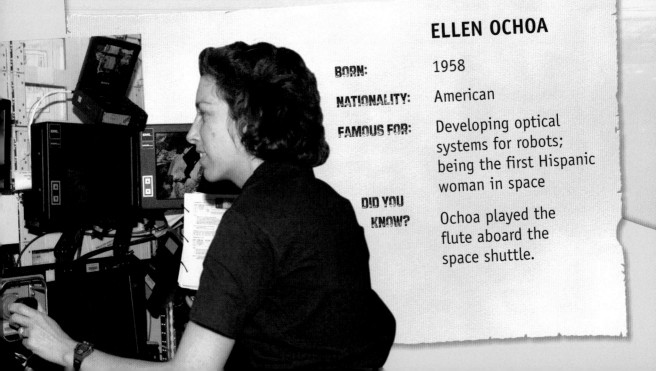

ELLEN OCHOA

BORN:	1958
NATIONALITY:	American
FAMOUS FOR:	Developing optical systems for robots; being the first Hispanic woman in space
DID YOU KNOW?	Ochoa played the flute aboard the space shuttle.

By controlling a robotic arm, Ochoa moved huge objects that became part of the International Space Station.

robotic arm

In the 1990s, Ochoa fulfilled her dream of becoming an astronaut. She spent over 900 hours in space on four missions of the **space shuttle**. Often she was in charge of the computers and robotic systems. In 1999 she controlled a robot arm that transferred goods and equipment from the space shuttle to the International Space Station. This was the first time such a feat had been attempted.

Later in her career, Ochoa studied the Sun's effects on Earth's atmosphere and the damage to ozone in the air. Ozone is a form of oxygen, and it collects high above the surface in the ozone layer. The ozone layer is important because it protects the surface from harmful radiation.

Today, Ochoa is the deputy director of the Johnson Space Center in Houston, Texas. She continues to help explore space and make new discoveries about space and Earth.

The SPACE RACE

For many years after World War II, the United States and the Soviet Union were fierce political rivals. The rivalry extended into space, too. Both countries competed to achieve their goals.

WERNHER VON BRAUN

Most scientists agree that the United States was able to launch rockets to the Moon in part because of the work of one man: Wernher von Braun. Von Braun is often called the father of rocket science.

Von Braun was born in Germany and worked to develop rockets there. After the end of World War II, the U.S. government recruited von Braun and many of his colleagues.

From 1969 to 1975, the United States landed 12 astronauts on the Moon. All returned safely to Earth.

Von Braun worked very hard to develop rockets, first for the U.S. military and then for NASA. His greatest achievement was developing the Saturn rockets that sent astronauts to the Moon. In 1975 he received the U.S. National Medal of Science.

QIAN XUESEN

Qian Xuesen (1911–2009) was born and raised in China. He went to the United States to study science and engineering. In the 1940s, he designed missiles and rockets for the U.S. Army. He also tried to design a type of airplane that could fly into space. Many years later, his work inspired the space shuttle.

By 1950, however, global politics affected Qian's career. Despite receiving support from many of his colleagues, Qian was barred from working for the military and came under suspicion because of his Chinese heritage. Eventually he left the United States and returned to China.

In China, Qian helped develop the Chinese space program. He also worked tirelessly to promote science education in China, often adapting the methods that he learned and practiced in the United States. In 2003 many of the students and scientists he inspired helped China launch its first astronauts into space.

Qian Xuesen (left) was visited by the Chinese head of government Wen Jiabao in August 2009.

EXPLORING SPACE TODAY

Today, everyone is benefiting from the work that began years ago. Satellites in orbit around Earth allow people to communicate rapidly, pinpoint their positions, and predict the weather. Telescopes in space have taken beautiful, detailed pictures of distant stars and galaxies. <u>Technology developed for space has been used to create everything from digital cameras to artificial limbs</u>.

Astronauts continue to travel to and from space. So do space probes, which carry equipment but not astronauts.

MICHAEL MEYER AND THE MARS EXPLORATION PROGRAM

Did life exist on Mars? If so, what was it like? These questions interest NASA scientist Michael Meyer. He is an astrobiologist, a scientist who studies the possibility of life in space. Currently he is in charge of the Mars Exploration Program, a series of missions that send space probes to Mars. Several space probes have landed on Mars, while others are in orbit around it.

Michael Meyer studied engineering, biology, and oceanography before becoming an astrobiologist.

Mars has no liquid water now, but it did have liquid water at some time in its past. Without liquid water, Mars cannot support living things. Meyer argues it could have been home to living things in the past. He and his team continue to look for evidence of Martian life. If those living things existed, they were very small and simple. They were more like Earth's ancient bacteria than its modern plants or animals.

In 2003 the space rovers Opportunity *(above) and* Spirit *revealed that Mars is red, rocky, and very cold.*

HUMANS ON MARS?

Many scientists and other experts believe that the next goal for space exploration should be sending astronauts to Mars. The return trip would be further than humans have ever traveled in space. It would take a year or longer. It would also be expensive and dangerous. Yet humans have always been explorers. A journey to Mars may happen in your lifetime.

THE SEARCH FOR EXTRATERRESTRIAL LIFE

Does life exist elsewhere in the universe, aside from Earth? Many people and organizations are searching for the answer to this question—which they hope is yes. The word *terrestrial* means "related to Earth." The search for extraterrestrial intelligence, or life away from Earth capable of thinking, is abbreviated as SETI.

One way to search for life in the universe is to visit different planets and moons and look for it. But the universe is enormous—far too vast to explore one planet at a time.

The people involved in SETI projects turn to radio telescopes to search for life. They listen for signs of intelligence, perhaps a radio or television program from a distant planet. To date, they have heard only static (background noise), but the search continues!

LESSONS FROM SPACE

The Sun, Moon, constellations, and other objects we see in the night sky have changed very little, if at all, since ancient times. But now we understand more about them and how they relate to Earth. We have even visited the Moon and sent space probes to other planets.

What lessons have we learned from studying space? Perhaps the most important lesson is that Earth, our home, is a very special place.

"The Earth is the only world known so far to harbor life. There is nowhere else, at least in the near future, to which our species could migrate. Visit, yes. Settle, not yet. Like it or not, for the moment the Earth is where we make our stand."

Carl Sagan, astronomer and author (1934–1996)

Astronauts from many nations serve aboard the International Space Station.

TIMELINE

Follow the colored arrows to see how some of the ideas and discoveries of astronomers influenced other scientists.

c. 147 CE

Ptolemy published the *Almagest*, a book about constellations and the movement of objects in space.

1609

Johannes Kepler published his first two laws of planetary motion. His third law was published ten years later.

1632

Galileo Galilei published a book in support of the Copernican system, and the Church denounced him.

c. 1000 CE

An observatory was built in the Mayan city of Chichén Itzá.

1543

Nicolaus Copernicus stated that planets revolve around the Sun, not Earth.

1687

Newton explained that gravity keeps planets in their orbits.

1925

Cecilia Payne-Gaposchkin showed that the Sun was made mostly of hydrogen.

1949

Fred Hoyle coined the term "Big Bang."

2009

The *Cassini* space probe discovered a new moon around Saturn, its seventh such discovery. *Galileo* had discovered Saturn's four largest moons.

1919

Edwin Hubble showed that the universe has many galaxies, not just the Milky Way. Later he showed that the galaxies are expanding.

1969

Astronauts Armstrong and Aldrin landed on the Moon and returned to Earth safely.

2006

The International Astronomical Union classified Pluto as a dwarf planet.

1910

Hertzsprung and Russell showed the relationship between the temperature and brightness of stars.

1992

Mather and Smoot discovered background radiation in space that is evidence for the Big Bang, the explosion that began the universe.

1994

Comet Shoemaker-Levy 9 crashed into Jupiter, showing the damage that collisions with objects from space can cause.

Quick Quiz

1 Which instrument can make distant objects appear closer?

(a) a microscope

(b) a telescope

(c) a television

2 Which subject is the scientific study of space?

(a) scientology

(b) astronomy

(c) astrology

3 Who believed that Earth was a fixed point in space?

(a) Copernicus

(b) Galileo

(c) Ptolemy

4 Where can you view images of stars and other objects in the sky?

(a) Madam Tussauds

(b) a natural history museum

(c) a planetarium

5 Which object from space is believed to have wiped out the dinosaurs on Earth?

(a) an asteroid

(b) a meteorite

(c) a comet

6 Who was the first person to receive a doctorate in astronomy from Harvard University?

(a) Carolyn Shoemaker

(b) Cecelia Payne-Gaposchkin

(c) Vera Rubin

7 Which scientist did not go to the United States to work?

(a) Wernher von Braun

(b) Andrei Sakharov

(c) Qian Xuesen

Answers: 1 (b), 2 (b), 3 (c), 4 (c), 5 (a), 6 (b), 7 (b)

Glossary

asteroid   rock, smaller than a planet, that is in orbit around the Sun

astronomy   scientific study of space and objects in space

astrophysicist   scientist who studies the physics or physical properties of objects in space

atmosphere   layer of gases that surrounds a planet

Big Bang   tremendous explosion that many scientists believe began the universe

black hole   extremely massive region of space from which nothing can escape

comet   mass of ice and dust in orbit around the Sun

constellation   group of stars that appears as a pattern in the night sky

dark matter   matter that is not visible but may account for observed forces of gravity

evidence   in science, observable facts from the natural world

galaxy   large group of stars within a region of the universe

gravity   attractive force between any two objects, such as the Sun and a planet

inertia   force that keeps an object moving or stopped until another force acts on it

NASA   National Aeronautics and Space Administration, the U.S. organization that conducts space exploration, scientific discovery, and aeronautics research

observatory   room or building for observing the sky and objects in space

phases   changing shapes of a planet or moon as viewed from Earth

planet   round, massive object that orbits the Sun or other star

radio telescope   type of telescope that uses radio waves to form images

radiation   energy in the form of heat or light sent out as invisible waves

revolve   move around, as a planet moves around the Sun

space shuttle   spacecraft made to take astronauts to and from space

space probe   robotic ship that explores space without astronauts, typically on missions that last many years

supernova   explosion of a massive star

telescope   tool that makes distant objects appear larger; used for observing objects in space

Find Out More

Books

Garlick, Mark A. *Atlas of the Universe* (Insiders). New York: Simon & Schuster Children's Publishing, 2008.

Gianopoulos, Andrea. *Isaac Newton and the Laws of Motion* (Graphic Inventions and Discovery). Chicago: Raintree, 2009.

Hibbert, Clare. *The Inside & Out Guide to Spacecraft*. Chicago: Heinemann Library, 2006.

Oxlade, Chris. *Gravity* (Fantastic Forces). Chicago: Heinemann Library, 2007.

Spilsbury, Richard and Louise. *Space Pioneers: Astronauts* (Scientists at Work). Chicago: Heinemann Library, 2008.

Stargazer's Guides. Chicago: Heinemann Library, 2007.

The Universe. Chicago: Heinemann Library, 2007.

Websites

Windows to the Universe
www.windows2universe.org
Visit this site to learn all about the solar system, stars, and galaxies. Each page is presented at three reading levels.

United States Naval Observatory
www.usno.navy.mil/USNO/astronomical-applications
Find links to astronomical information from the United States Naval Observatory in Washington, DC.

The Royal Observatory, England
www.nmm.ac.uk/places/royal-observatory
Review exhibits on space and space exploration at the Royal Observatory in London, England.

Women in Astronomy
www.kidscosmos.org/kid-stuff/women-astro.html
Read about women who have made and are making amazing
contributions to astronomy.

NASA
www.nasa.gov/audience/forstudents/index.html
This NASA website for students has useful information to do with space
and NASA's space exploration.

Places to visit

Adler Planetarium
1300 South Lake Shore Drive
Chicago, IL 60605
Tel: 312-922-7827
www.adlerplanetarium.org

The Adler was founded in 1930 as America's first planetarium.

Smithsonian National Air and Space Museum
National Air and Space Museum on the National Mall
6th and Independence Avenue, SW
Washington, DC 20560
Tel: 202-633-1000
www.nasm.si.edu

See the Apollo 11 command module that carried astronauts to the Moon
and back, and touch a sample of Moon rock.

Griffith Observatory
2800 East Observatory Road
Los Angeles, CA 90027
Tel: 213-473-0800
www.griffithobservatory.org

Visit this public observatory operated by the City of Los Angeles.

Index

antimatter 33
asteroids 16, 17
astrology 9
astronauts 35, 37, 38, 39, 41
astronomy 9
astrophysics 14, 27

Big Bang 15, 30, 31, 32, 33
black holes 23, 30
Braun, Wernher von 36–37
Brown, Beth 27

Catholic Church 10, 11
Chandra telescope 26, 27
Chandrasekhar, Subrahmanyan 23, 27
Chichén Itzá 5, 42
comets 16, 17, 43
constellations 6, 7
Copernican Revolution 8–9
Copernicus, Nicolaus 8, 9, 10, 42
Cosmic Background Explorer (COBE) 32

dark matter 25
dwarf planets 18, 19

Earth 7, 8, 11, 12, 14, 16, 17, 21
eclipses 14
Enceladus 29
expansion of the universe 24, 30, 32
extrasolar planets 29
extraterrestrial life 29, 38, 39, 40

Frail, Dale 29

galaxies 14, 24, 25
Galileo Galilei 10–11, 27, 29, 42
gas giants 29
gravity 11, 12–13, 17, 30, 32

Hawking, Stephen 10, 30–31
Hayden Planetarium 15
helium 20, 32
Hertzsprung, Ejnar 22, 43
Hoyle, Fred 31, 43
Hubble, Edwin 24, 30, 43
Hubble Space Telescope 25, 28
hydrogen 20, 32

inertia 12
International Astronomical Union (IAU) 18
International Space Station 34, 35, 41

Jodrell Bank 4
Johnson Space Center 35
Jupiter 11, 16, 17, 29

Kepler, Johannes 13, 42

laws of motion 12

Mars 38–39
Mather, John 32, 43
matter 21, 25, 32
Meyer, Michael 38–39
microwaves 27
Milky Way 24
models of the universe 7, 9, 11
Moon 10, 11, 14
Moon landings 36, 43
moons 11, 29

National Aeronautics and Space Administration (NASA) 17, 27, 32, 34, 37
Neptune 16, 29
Newton, Isaac 12, 13, 42

Ochoa, Ellen 34–35
optical telescopes 27
orbits 12, 13, 18
Orion constellation 6
ozone layer 35

Payne-Gaposchkin, Cecilia 20–21, 43
phases 10
planets 7, 9, 12, 13, 14, 16, 18, 29
plasma 21
Pluto 18–19, 29, 43
Porco, Carolyn 29
Ptolemy 7, 9, 42
pyramids 5

Qian Xuesen 37

radiation 5, 32, 35
radio telescopes 4, 5, 40
radio waves 5, 27
red giants 23
rockets 36–37
Rubin, Vera 25
Russell, Henry 22, 43

Sagan, Carl 23, 40
Sakharov, Andrei 33
satellites 38
Saturn 11, 29
science fiction 27, 31
SETI projects 40
Shoemaker, Carolyn 16
Smoot, George F. 32, 43
solar system 14, 16
space exploration 34–39
space probes 11, 26, 29, 38, 43
Space Race 36–37
space shuttles 35, 37
stars 5, 6, 14, 20, 21, 22–23, 24, 25, 28, 29, 32
Stern, Alan 18, 19
Sun 7, 8, 9, 11, 12, 20, 21, 23
sunspots 11
supergiants 22, 23
supernovas 23, 28, 32

Tancredi, Gonzalo 19
telescopes 4, 5, 10, 11, 25, 26–27, 38, 40
Tombaugh, Clyde 19
Tyson, Neil Degrasse 14–15

Uranus 29

Venus 10

white dwarfs 22, 23
Wolszczan, Aleksander 29
women astronomers 16, 20–21, 25, 27, 29, 34–35

X-rays 27